Byssus

Jen Hadfield

Byssus

PICADOR

First published 2014 by Picador
an imprint of Pan Macmillan, a division of Macmillan Publishers Limited
Pan Macmillan, 20 New Wharf Road, London N1 9RR
Basingstoke and Oxford
Associated companies throughout the world
www.panmacmillan.com

ISBN 978-1-4472-4110-2

A CIP catalogue record for this book is available from the British Library.

Printed and bound by CPI Group (UK) Ltd, Croydon, CR0 4YY

Visit **www.picador.com** to read more about all our books
and to buy them. You will also find features, author interviews and
news of any author events, and you can sign up for e-newsletters
so that you're always first to hear about our new releases.

Contents

to the dear folk

Lichen

Who listens
like lichen listens

assiduous millions of black
and golden ears?

You hear

      and remember

but I'm speaking
to the lichen.

The little ears prunk,
scorch and blacken.

The little golden
mouths gape

Saturday Morning

It's always false spring somewhere and most of all in your
brain with its painful thaws. Get up and away from it — to
milk from the freezer blown up into a yellow bagpipe: a
rimed stone splitting its sides and burning your palms. To
sun broaching the salt-blurred windows. To live cockles in
brine, mumbling sand and bubbled spires of mucus. At least
half of you's still below the surface, probing the pillow with
xylem fingers, and so wishing for a body to match yours that
you would even love your enemy, who for fuck's sake *holds*
you, when you meet in this dream.

the cockle's smile
Smiles learnt in the cockle-beds

is an ambiguous
smile

a brackish
smile

a sidling
smile

a conservative
smile

a dole
smile

a self-centred
smile

a stuck-in-the-
mud smile

a salad-days
smile

a gummy
smile

a scare-yourself
smile

a spit-in-your-
eye smile

a tough-nut-
to-crack smile
    a philosopher-
waving-his-quodlibet-
of-wrack smile

                        a Smeagol
smile

      a survival
smile

a final
smile

      a fossil

              smile

We climb the hill in the dark and the children are finally given back their iPhones

...mid-sentence, Kusra,
bravening, detaches
her humid paw
from mine, swept up

like a ripened copepod
in a current of complaint
and omniscient
App-light. To avert

the dirty, natural night,
they've cracked open
their phones like geodes:
dazzled we stream

through the wedged ruts
and cowpats, fishing
for a signal or satellite.
Mum, I'm safe, I've got

six bars! Shaniya
touched egg-blood!Miss –
get back into the line
of light! And finally

attempt to take pics
of the stars, of dark
country lanes, of the hot
perturbation of Sirius.

The March Springs

scraps of rabbit

stomachy moss

masses

of the tender, green lungy stuff

the warm snow at your neck

skylarks going up like flares

mucus blown from your nostrils spit

or spirit from your sore throat

running downhill t

o the cockle-beds

as if you'd just been born a

lamb

It's impossible to think of any one thing – Spring a hybrid
God, Gosh or Gum: dewlap bulging, bugling with glory;
spring-steam rolling off the whale-backed hill. Screws
sparkling in the grass, the brand of a steel rule. He's going to
break himself all day: hammering and knocking out nails,
sawing and bracing and using the old words.

*

The light's like powdered glass. Sparrows'-wings like shuffled
cards and Mexican chirps we can't spell in our language. The
sharp, white breeze is Mexican, but if I tried to describe the
smell of the air, I'd have to hood the vowels with hyphens,
the gods being in the vowels. Are you hereabouts in your
stocking feet? Look at the state of me. Various pietà attitudes:
head rolling like an erratic; knees shoved up to the sun's
stove. Trying to be everywhere at once. The smell of burning
cedar and there are no cedars. The smell of pines and there
are no pines. Everywhere rubs up against the islands; the
archipelago strains everywhere through its teeth. It takes two
days to begin to write fluently, and I've got one. One day to
begin to write, and then off into town as a Mexican saint,
with my eyes on a dish and heart unpacked from its ruddy
conglomerate.

*

When spring comes it's all too bright and spiteful: blinding
sky, blinding sea, daffodil shaws and laverick song. So I shut
my eyes and spoot out my neck and hoop it like a swan and
arch it for the blinding, bright-white sun to bite and smile
the 'sex-starved smile'.

The Memory of Timber

by want –
as in 'I want you' and

'I want to write' – I mean
as if the sap in the floorboards candled

and began to flow – bruises freshening
round the cleats and congealed grain

loosening like lava around the nails and knots
to giddy in lees where flour-gold would gather

were floorboards a river

I want –

no wonder the cat skips and shivers
and stares up wildly

into empty corners –

the knots scorch the shirred flesh
in their readiness

to spout scaled limbs –
the knots are the shape of sparrows'

breasts puffed up against
a snow-strafed wind

The Black Hole

A ring of down-feathers surrounds the corpse
of the blackbird, thickly leaved like pages
of a burnt book. The cat steels himself at
their stirring perimeter. I've seen him
biff a robin's carcass to make it look
lively, crunching into the ginger-nut
of its breast, but he seems to teeter on
the brink of the blackbird – the breezy shiv–
er of charred down-feathers – that eye,
a scuffed sequin of blood. If the fallout
stirs, he smacks his lips, as he does when he
perceives a threat. His flanks palpitate, star–
ing down into the black hole by mistake.

The Ambition

after Rabelais

*The tide being out, I'd to traipse through dehydrated eelgrass
and the chopped warm salad of the shallows, and then the
Atlantic breached me part by part.*

If my knees knocked it was two flints striking
My skin shagreen
My thorax a corset compressed rib by rising rib
My fingerprints finely-carved trilobites of the shore
My fine motor skills as good as any butterwort's
My nail-beds pale flukes: lemon soles or witches
My blood a thick slow scrawl of crude
If seals mobbed the shallows, it was only for my liver
If my kidneys complained, they were Bert and Ernie
My throat a maypole for eel-grass
My retinas red rags to bulls
A raw kebab, my vertebrae strung on the spinal cord
My nose and ears sympathetic remora
My pigtail a withered stipe or shaw
My moles and freckles rising spores
If I floated it was spatch-cock, trussed on the swell
If I expressed myself well, it was liquids and vowels
My musculature like dispersing cirrus
My sweat-glands like mud-buried lugworms
My children a cloud of clumped alfabeti
My urine a strong, hot tisane

If my knuckles were cracked, it was for their chilled marrow
My lips and tongue seasoned by an infinite cruet
My sphincters the knots in a balloon poodle
My brain-pan a shovel of quenched ash
My cerebellum a bait-ball
The full moon the most serious in a season of crushes
My slack my hammock
My plankton my inattention
My ghost pots my amnesia for names and faces
My luciferins my name in lights
My name sticks and sinking stones
My littoral my high-disclosure zone
My breadcrumb sponge my ephemeral path home

The Murder Stone

1. Desire path

Reap the high pith
which sweeps the meek
along –

mangroves of sunday
and tortoiseshell, the bog's
blithe nymph

pishing
through misshapens:
tall Aspergers, Parson-grass

and Fitting Orchis
breach a warble-wall
of rusky iron.

2. Ear-worm

Hate: knee-deep weather; cuckold spit and span;
that wedding march, that meddling song

working my what-like
a wig-worm.

3. Golf-course

Trundling a tameness,
spraying their pocked roe,

unpursing it from tender caddies as if to split it
with the stick and spray it with the milt —

we've weirder ways
to fertilise.

4. Ootadaeks

Berks, darlings,
and debbie-call-em
horse-cures.

Bops implode
from the hearkening.

Thoughtfully, the sea's
lift-offish vacancies,

blurred with fetch
and carry.

The White Goods

Emptying the freezer. Using up the
wonton skins, the last of the piltocks,
the mackerel fillets in their oily lamé,
the   salmon-heads   and   galangal.
Defrosting it. Chipping the fluted scales
of choux annealed in a frozen slick;
detaching the magnets; hoovering the
shaggy grille that regarded the wall,
waltzing its dark face to the light.
Disclosing sodden, black curds, the
immaculately-preserved   Wheat
Crunchie which turns out to be an
earplug. I endlessly recover infinite
planes, the inanimate taint on the
plastic panes where the two worlds war
over their shared frontier. Their frost-
pelts crawl all over each other; the
glacial brow has doubled over the door.
Our rinds fray and sift down around us
and settle continually like marine snow.

Hydra

For D & S & F & A & L

Were we like a plough, ancient or modern,
or a plough like us – as you taught us to *dell*,

to dig as digging used to be done
the four of us side by side, and moving as one

along each new row and down the fallowed yard?
Straining to turn the chunked soil,

we intermittently fell into a genius rhythm:
trod the spade-heads, and teetered while you cut

the corner of the clod; raising our blades
in the fissure to turn the dead weight

of it together and then striking
the same, rolled clod in unison

with spades honed to a thin, ragged edge,
as cobras with their hoods spread dash

from the same knot of muscle.
Just as often I whacked one

of you with my hip or arse or our hat-brims clashed
or the spade just missed the hand that darted

into turned earth for docken root or shards of lim
or we eyed Foula, distant

in blue haze, and panted, or hosed the pig,
who shuddered the water from her curling bristles

and tacked about her park. We filled our hats
at the tap and worked on with earlobes dripping,

while the dryness washed down from our first row,
the turned roots parching in the sun,

until it was done,
in the cooling of the light.

Ruined Croft, with Listening Station

after *On the Tilt, Perthshire,* Edwin Henry Landseer, 1826

The unfaithful act of composition:

to frame the lintel and folksy bruck
around the fallen gaevil — laem,
cow's jaw, yoag-shell, poison bottle —

you crop out the long rustle of airspace,
the green dome of the listening station,
old relay installations, all those relics

of the Cold War; kye licking salt from
their crumbling walls. And seem to
dispossess both dead and the living:

all the dear folk, in their high-visibility
outerwear. Louis firing his NERF gun.
You and me rough-and-tumbling down

the hill at the risk of cracking ribs.
Sour gusts of heat and perfume from
the stirred earth. A span of sea glittering

with gannets, like a face-full of piercings.

The Wedding Road, with Free Bar

after *A Highland Wedding,* copper plate printed on cotton

So
you and
I

chum
each other ever slow

er up
the winding road
until we lie dow
n   on its friend
ly tar, grasping our brok
en dahlias

while the con
nsternations

park
thems
elves.

In Revolution Politics Become Nature

after Ian Hamilton Finlay

A SNEEZING SHERIFF · TH

ROAT STACKED WITH C

HINS · PELT SPOTTED WIT

H MAYORAL DAPPLES · R

EPRESENTATIVE OF TH

E SILENT MAJORITY THE

DARK GREY NATION IN

THE KELPBEDS · THE SHA

DOW CABINET OF SEALS

The Jinx

You cast into the wind.

There were no fish
surely there were no fish anywhere
just the shore ringed

with moon jellies
a violet nebula stranded and spun
by the current.

I said *I think I'm a jinx.*
You said *I think you might be.*
You picked a hook

from a little sillock's gill
chucking it back to cast
again. The mild carousel

of jellyfish
plied the surface from
the open sea

almost
inaudibly rising
and falling

Da Coall

'tae-girse, tormentil;/whitna tapestry for a killin field'
– Christine De Luca, 'Da Coall'

Sundew

Does this place look to you
like the cusp of never
and nothing and nowhere?

Look down into the encampment
of the blanket bog. It flushes
as it sweats out round-leaved sundew:

gold-panning, double-
bunking, a mass of dew-
blinged eyes. They just spread

their sticky fingers to get back
in the black; close them
on a fortune of tiny flies.

Butterwort

Forget the day's *eye*.
The bog's an erogenous zone
baroqued by a million Gaudís –
wave upon wave of zany
nano-blooms proffering
their tender meat-and-two-
veg to the air. I've fallen
to my knees again not five
minutes from home: first,
the boss of Venusian leaves
that look more like they docked
than grew; a sappy nub;
violet bell; the minaret
of purpled bronze. And
milkwort, gentian, asphodel,
a Sistine ceiling of flowers.

Spring Squill

What does spring cost
the blanket bog?
The thin-skinned

rabbit knows –
tunnelling down into
mantel and core –

dead-end of
earth-fast rock –
starve/rest –

and surface
here,
very, heart

hammering, in a streaming
mirage of *scilla verna,* migraine
of tormentil.

The Finns

for Davy Cooper

'persons [...] possessed of the Finnish art could perform feats
by sea or water quite impossible to ordinary mortals [...] could
render themselves visible or invisible at pleasure [and] metamorphose
themselves into the likeness of beast, bird, or fish.'
– John Spence, *Shetland Folklore*

Now the eyes
become as big
as bees

with the property
of seeing

through their
own lids.

When, in the shallows
between sleep
and waking,

you discover in
your jaw a curved
yellow tooth,

narrow
as a canula,

it's a clue
to what

you might
be becoming.

The Puffballs

(the pursed turf
blowing bubbles)

        (a broken string
        of irregular pearls,
        packed with cool,

                white roe;
              the flesh that fries
              to a savoury foam
)

(a female smell
on your fingers)

          (they
        roost on their
        tethers of fine,
        private hair)
              (glimmer
              in the dark—
                ening)

     (ripening
     in their
     sockets)

                    its anchor and bowls
                 forever brewing buboes, it slips
              blackened blowhole; toxic stoma. A toff
           a pocked sphincter;
        this gassy urn of moolah. Its gob gapes:
     their yellow teeth this amph of moorit smoke,
        of blinding business. Sheep assay with
              nova it squats, rocking its stoor
                 A faux pas, unsuper

                                          the

              cliff-

                   top

                                              in
                        g

           s

                   o r

across

hicc!

upp

out

its

p

e

s

Quartz

after Eeva Kilpi

As the light relaxes its hold
I will continue in the valley
to lather, like two chunks
of soap, quartz
between my palms,
while dim moths settle
on dim cushions
of campion.

The milky faces of the mineral
shear together, flint forth
claret sparks, like fireflies.

Don't tell me, if you know
how it happens.

Puffballs

for Lotte Glob & The Loch Eriboll Chorus

You Mork eggs —
you Finns, you eyeless
Dia de Muertos
skulls — how
do you and your
nation grow?

Are you
peripatetic,
rolled about the cliffs
until the music stops,
when each lets down
a frail plait?

Or the moon
herds you up
through the mold
like little white bulls,
forcing the walls
of the *kyunnen's*
burrow

.

When I wake on the cliff, with heart beating down
on the thin, dungy soil, and waves seeming to break

inside me, I would just like to know what lies
between belly and bedrock. I know how securely

the cliff clasps you and that to touch
with lips is like nuzzling a kneecap.

To snack on you – sheepish – where you grow
is like eating *löragub*, sea-haze, expanding foam.

To sniff your socket in the grass
is to recall some humid porch of the body.

To explore it with my tongue
very saucy, grass tickling my chin.

Your tanned hide is already
the colour of a bog burial's skin, bronzed

and thin, half-hollow now, but tough but
perforated neatly by a raindrop

.

and you live
to sing to blurt

your spore-mass
from your ragged

moue!
O pepperpot

lift up
your voice! –

for the wind
to broadcast,

like smoke,
like spice.

Definitions

after Jerome Rothenberg

The Brisket

This cinched consonant, hunched muscle in a yellow
simmet, could also signify a journey. It could feed a family,
or stop the third gob of the three-headed dog. You bind it
to your stick as you set off for the Underworld. Browned, it
melts into punctuated mud, is thick fuel for migrations,
night flights you can't remember. It's a passing madness in
the cat; it makes him a round-eyed bawling bob-cat. It
squirms under the distal phalanges of a splayed hand. It
bucks the bite of the knife. It foams fat.

The Cat

is sleeping very deeply now it's spring been off his head
hunting rabbits all night, in the far-out stones and discoball
eyes of the clifftop crö. His days a kind of stoned remission:
heart-beat irregular, muscles leaping violently in sleep. The
wet bracelet of his mouth unlatched; chattering a little; his
eyelids half-open. His furry buffers nicely spread all about
him; nicely buffered by fat and fur all round.

Equus Primus

as if some god having turned out another batch of
underdone horses (thin as leaves, dappled like leaves) freed
them on the hill to flicker like a thicket of hornbeam and
willow; set down his cutter and balled the waste dough.
Thence this tribe of blackened emoticons, tough as plugs.

The Word 'Died'

It's a cliff-sided stack: sheer, almost an island. A human
can't stand upon that high, tilted pasture but life crowds its
cliffs: sheep and nesting maas, the waste-not plants of
heath and moor. You hear the waves breaking but can't see
them. You shrink down into yourself as you reach the edge:
getting your head around where you are. It's marvellous.
It's aweful. It is always on. Like a massive *and* unfolding its
wings, and mantling. It was here all along, reached by
Shirva and the derelict mills; turf sweating in the hot,
midgy smirr.

The Mackerel

At once, the three hooks chime. The skin is as supple as the
skin on boiled milk and the eye a hard, roundel pane. It is
or it isn't wormy, it tastes of hot blood and earth, tastes of
long-awaited rain, winter lightning and summer thunder.
Heart-throb; mud-coloured; the cooked flesh is tarnish. The
oatmeal crisp. It tastes of steak, it tastes of cream.

The Northern Lights

– but yes, now you pull over – after the headlights, a raw
shifting glare. I've taken them often for a moon behind
cloud. An ambiguous rustling, yes, maybe listening in, when
being overheard is your greatest fear. Like an infection of the
lymph, a shooting-up – that single, white flare.

The Orange

Bloated, swollen with sea-water, it's a boast, fraught with
salt syrup. It forces your fingers apart and makes much of
itself. It is über, *aaber*. A very straining round real orange,
stinking of orange and the sea; stinking of stale cologne.
The sea returns whatever you give it, more so, realler.
Headachy wax! It rolls down the sand into the foam. It
spins at the crest of the breaker!

The Parents

are on the pale brisk longbusy birdbrushed billows of the
equinoctial sea. Without them is a long, unhappy holiday.
Who else gives a shit about your shitty knee? You're
breathless at the thought of them all-night on the sea.
Blithely they step into its bright pale machinery. They
make mandalas of quartz and limpet-shells, hide cash under
a hairbrush, vanish with their luggage as pixies might. The
pillows squared to each other. The sheets pulled tight.

The Pig

is as they say, very human, though our bellies do not
resemble her belly, which is like one of the papyriform
columns at Luxor. Nor can we liken our nipples to her
torment of buttons, our ears to her arums. Our lugs are
unfringed with soft, blonde baleen. But her fetishes: her
forked stick; her devilish loop of rotted rope. Her precious
rasher of chicken wire. Her tired, human eye. Her
constancy as a conspirator.

The Puffballs

Somebody's watching. Two toughened eyeballs propped
behind you on the turf.

The Puffin

A tangled marionette, strings of jerked sinew. Summer's
end, the derelict burrow, a ring of dirty down. An
arabesque of smelly bone, meat for flies and the darling
turf. The head may be full of meat; the large beak, faded: a
Fabergé egg.

The Road to the North Light

It weeps tar from tender parts like frogskin. Thin, mobile muscles squirm under your soles as it bears you across the Hill Dyke on a current of cool air, the bed of an invisible river. It has heather and tormentil, not dandelion but catsear. It has a creep over a precipice; it has sorrel, parched and tiny. It carries you above the white and lilac sea; it switchbacks, and turns you before the sun like a sacrifice.

The Slater

We alone among the creatures are known to imagine our own minds. Like this woodlouse on the kitchen floor. It perceives you, rears and comes about. Stroking with its spurred feet a precipitate of dried soup, a peel hovering above its own shadow.

The Waxcaps

Someone was carried across this field, bleeding steadily.

Five Mackerel

for Mary

Here's something
we can begin
to get our heads
around unlike

her summer
leaving

your kitchen
the unexpected
 mackerel

potato salad
with spring onion
big chunks
of apple

the hot, spitting fish
split easily
with the back
of the knife

opened
along its rig
the pinbones
drawn out.

And then
for the contrast
the boiled chunks
with just a *scar*

of vinegar
almost
a dessert
of fish

the cold tap
run over them.

In Memoriam

'No metaphors swarm

around that fact, around that strangest thing,
that being that was and now no longer is.'

— Iain Crichton Smith

I

For it is not like a sea of nested gas
that you float upon
in your pedalo.

This unspeakable is not *like*
anything

a poem or riddle collies no particle
of it for us to fank
in mouths and minds.

A noun's a nickname
and makes it *reestit*

adjectives salt, parch and wizen it.
Language abdicates

but you
in your stocking feet
stand a chance

with your long-lost primer
of liquids and vowels.

II

Loving language is wide
and shallow: sooks, polches
and wistens it.

Already I can only noun
about its shores
and surfaces

nym the brinks of this squilly thing

where congregates stuff
that can be likened:

stiff hands like ginger root
in the dim, summer night;

the kettle's glossy coat of tar;
the little flame of the driftwood fire

bunched
and clerical.

III

First we'll need
to agree:

are we taking up the first language
or must we coin
a new one?

If we're going to speak about this
I'll need a tinderbox and tent
and waterskin.

We will need to use the nights
as fully as the nesting birds.

The Thin Places

this place
these folk

what was on your doorstep
all along

is only bared gradually,
as it could be borne,

as the Clift Hills clear
through bright black

spiders'-nests of fog –
each death the moult

of another thin layer.
You weren't prepared

for this you hadn't met
your nearest neighbour

but even as fog poured
over the cliffs again,

late light disclosed
the Neolithic wall.

You found a message
on the answering machine –

it's just me –
wishin dee well.

Birches and maples

Some of us are birches and maples, and don't need any help
to cry. They weep without noticing. They cry without
shame, asleep or waking – a tear like a twisted root shoves
lustily into an ear. And the syrup of the fluent birch boils
down to next-to-nothing.

Others are arid: wetten most effortfully. They say *I could
weep* – fighting for custody of each concentrated tear.
Crying them is as arduous as milking ewes, or harvesting
saffron. The world bulges as if it'll burst, but becomes
clear.

The Plinky-Boat

'the present is a fine line [...]a puff of air would destroy it'
– Gaspar Galaz, 'Nostalgia de la Luz'

Something near to true
night-darkness. The children
are playing the Plinky-Boat –
a xylophone made
from a reclaimed yoal –
built for flexibility in a coarse
sea, you can tell it fledged
with ease, just blushed
from boat to instrument,
transpiring streams
of these hoarse night-
notes. For its copper pipes
are cut to breadth exactly
so the boat's beam is
its sotto voce and two rills
of rising pitch run into
the harmonic of each
hinnyspot – where
the boards of gunwales
and stem flow together.
I don't know what it is
about this place that things
metaflower so readily
into their present selves.

The instrument's a boat,
the notes unresonant
and scales of thin light
swarm over the pipes
from the boys' headtorches.
Perhaps we heard seals
broaching in the harbour
as they answered the girls
' handclapping game –
I doubt they moaned
in their haunted wise –
here was everything –
words lost, as I'm trying
to say, their echo, that
yodel into past and future.
The poem wouldn't exist,
but we couldn't stay.

You were running a bath, and being Gulliver

– on your index finger was a moth, a sort
of minute circus bear, delicately wiped
from the sweating tiles,
whose nano-drag on the ball
of the digit
was the weight and heft of a pheromone,
a living placebo.

It had tacked its invisible crampons
into your fingerprint's mazed whorls
with a barely-discernable
pain. Its back-combed beehive
of tawny fur
thickened to a grizzly's ruff; a compass
and its arc described

in the wing's dust-art of shaded triangles
and intersecting lines; twinned, symmetrical
coffee-coloured dots.
It was something about a friend
that threw you off-
kilter, one of those ambiguities or
loopholes in what we owe each other,

you'd sat so long that enough Lilliputian
bubbles had gathered in your body-hair
to launch you up into
the trade-winds. Though the tiny steed stamped
you couldn't feel
it, though it shivered the eloquent
flakes of its wings.

The Asterism

'a mystery, and a waste of pain'
– Annie Dillard

Inexplicable pain –
you're a thing like Sirius
or Aldebaran – another
asterism of the first magnitude:
remote incandescence –
colour – heat – which degrade
when I regard you with
the naked eye, dazzling
and extinct.

When I consider all
the things you are – the neglect
of pain; a window of slumping glass
between us and the distorted world –
I wish we held you not inside
but near. Jungled

in your orchid
and passionflower,
creepers and bromeliads
of pain, we'd peer through
each other's scintillate leaves.

If we spoke of you at all,
it was ruefully,
to say:

If it flowered
less often, like a cactus,
then I might look forward
to its alien bloom. Still,
when it dies back, I feed
and pot it up.

Or boast *I grafted*
and grew a great pain
last year, a scion
of the original
stock.

The Kids

Born too soon,
Monday's child was unready to be seen;
is destined to be early for ever.

She's selected a slice of red pepper
shaped
like a question mark.

*

The volcanic breath of Tuesday's child!
He remembers where poetry comes from;
the literal potential of things,

which means he can't eat broccoli —
seeing it right, a tiny indigestible oak.

He eats grated cheese with a teaspoon,
assisting it with a finger.

*

The hidden's the vocation of bird-like Wednesday's child,
perfecting her dust-baths with sweeping boughs of pine.

She can find anything hidden in the dark,
as a cat finds a rabbit —

by steam escaping
the warren.

*

Thursday's child says he saw Wednesday's child
run so fast she began to fly.

Thursday's child shall be called a liar.

*

Friday is afraid of the suit of spades
and jigsaw pieces the shape of the suit of spades.

She's afraid of plug-sockets, pylons,
dams, flowered wallpaper.

She knows what magic is —
the stress we're under.

*

Saturday's child is still growing into her eyes
(lamps above her chin, a frog's eyes surfacing

the muds of winter).
She can't help what she does and doesn't see —

salting away what she sees
inside her.

*

Sunday's child knows what blasphemy is
and where the devil's grave.

He makes the lovely graves
of long grass and speedwell.

Gloriana

for F

Gloriana, whose shoulders are cannon, whose lugs are
swivelling swamp-lilies sump enough to sink a fist, to our
trusty and well-beloved servant –
          Greeting.

Has our servant brought a bale of straw? For currency falls
from the sovereign bum. By these our presents we
diligently enrich the auric straw, doubling it in weight and
worth. Then, sums done, together – even as close as twins
in utero – we'll circle each other in the sty, tear the thick
pages of the bale and shake the authentic integers out, and
plunge amongst the airy floes of nones and ones, and you
shall rest against the royal bellypork, and scratch the
bearded royal jaw, which recalls The Tudor.

Break the bank now, strew the straw! For approaches the
hour we like to tilt our delicate nouse, that intelligent
scrying cup, to the skies above our kingdom. We think this
a golden age we do not go to war nor fare the many pages
nor portion out the inordinate indigos. Above the suave hill
rise wonders – equivocating ideograms of geese, the
brimming pothole we dub our 'moon.' Your sovereign shall
be your interpreter.

But now our well-beloved servant must withdraw. We have our art at night, when the heavy work of state is done. We press straw to stone for the midwinter sun to light, as it falls to its knees at the threshold of our sty. We call these crushed bright ikons *'Straw, on Stone.'*

Hairst

Like a snore in the sinus
of Russian comfrey, a slowing
orange drummie-bee

*

Under the flowering currant,
the two cats' mummering mystery play.
Slow-motion pawfall

*

The sun reaches the back wall.
My sparrow nib tosses aside
wet leaves of shadow

*

Moon a bashed swede.
I cut a way into the prickly core
of the dogroses.

Black bouquets: hollow stalks, rattling pods.
The secateurs are broken: their blades cross-
bill, twisted out of true

*

Ringing unanswered on the cliff,
like an old black bakelite
phone, the raven

*

Gate like a chapped mouth,
that the wind picks
and peels, gate that droops outwards

like a broken wing and utters
until it's empty, giving
and giving

*

Is yun Mammy's glivs?
Well, yes, what's left of them,
web-frail, held

together these seven
years by a fused mass
of darns

*

To know your place:
a doorstep amongst the floating
islands

*

The sky thin as cuticle and
moon a gash into the light beyond
a rime of scarlet at her prow

*

The wind's always got to be the dame
in a ten-gallon hat
fake fruit and flowers overflowing

*

The children say *I'm dead,*
lying on their backs
on wet concrete; leap up;

cross the playground heel
-to-toe, hoist the blue gym mats
to catch the gale

*

Soon the sun
shines through
the warren

A Very Circular Song

At the brink of the cliff the boy on the quadbike
goes round and around the crag at the geo,
the bull in the ring of his own making
and the halfmoon Nissen huts are lit
and their doors rolled back
on bright trowie-halls in the hill.

And the wind turns like a great water-wheel
coming from the north to pad briefs
on the line with pudenda of the wind
which someone would need to take in
before the next shower, or leave them drenched
to dry again. And gales are followed

by rare, clear days and steady, cold nights,
like tankers to tow the next gale in.
More or less crucially, across the isles,
these acts exceed themselves, like trout-mouthings;
the cement mixer baying at the daylight moon,
the leg-hobbled, baby-faced Texel tup

scoring a dial in the sodden yard
as the boy on the quad goes round
and around the same crag
tearing the trembling bog with his tyres,
the headlight and the tail-light
at the brink of the geo.

Ceps

The going
is a moon-walk
over springy terraces
of ice-shattered rock, riddled
with arctic scramblers,
bearberry and minute
mountain azalea, sunspots
through fog, an occasional blaze
of sea below – all
battened down and
buttoned up except
this mushroom, like a piece
of vernacular furniture,
tough droiltin tree
that seems to sprout
from the language of heart
and hearth; massy corbel
of the least willow. It's not
sex I'm trying to get my head
around but what our
flowering costs us
I'm afraid that in this
as ever we spend
beyond our means. Who'd
jut out a poem except
they were in love?
The human way is ever

unsustainable –
whatever we make –
we wax more
and more outlandishly
beautiful until luminous our skin
splits; the scrambling twig
herniates its varnished bole,
well, yes, a gargoyle,
a hard-on.

Bardifield

After your tale
I expected to hear revenants
in the wind

but it was only such chat
as might catch across the water
on a still night,

men chewing the fat
at cattle-grids, in passing places,
elbow on the sill

of a wound-down
window: low-key, mutterous,
satisfied spirits.

The Session

A ring of
men doubled
over the bellyache
of their guitars looking
at anything but
each other but
mostly at
the backs
of their eyelids –
muddy hide where
blood patterns the
flamelight – hand
-prints and
aurochs
and leaping and
running men
and boars.
The tune's the
thing they're
nursing, a
smoored ember
they carry from camp
to camp, shielding
it from the wind
and fanning
for dear life its
fitting, mossy flame.

Lighting tune from
tune like this through
the later days
infinitely
bigging the
round house
of music
with no
door.

The Moult

Stay out of the sun:
we can all see you. Stop picking fights
above your weight. We've this high

golden bowl of heather and moss
company of whaups and cries and
mutters in the wind; the long

draught of islands

and blinding sea.

Shelter in the hoodoos and pluck
your fur – fine smelt caught on heather
and shining reeds –

ruing it as I do, this flying
gleaming floss snatched back
and spent by the wind.

Freeze when the sunlight hits you

you're not invisible. Scratch off

your dreamcoat of silver money.
Rest downwind in the sun. Run
double-jointed when the valley dims.

Shetland Words

aaber – keen, eager

bruck – rubbish

crö, or *crub* – drystone enclosure for sheep or crops

dee – you (second person singular)

drummie-bee – bumblebee

flukes – flatfish

gaevil – gable of a house

hairst – autumn

kye – cows

kyunnen – rabbit

laverick – skylark

laem/lemm – earthenware/crockery

lum – chimney

maa – general term for a seagull

moorit – dark brown fleece

ootadaeks – outside the hill-dykes. John J. Graham adds this note: 'Used occasionally in a metaphorical sense to indicate place occupied by a human which was not his normal place of abode.'

piltock – coalfish two to four years old

scar – a dash

shalder – oystercatcher. In his *Icelandic Journal* of 1871, William Morris recounts how Faulkner shoots some oystercatchers 'on a venture' and serves them for dinner, noting that in Iceland they are known as 'tjalder'.

spoot – razor clam

tirricks – Arctic terns

whaup – curlew

yoal – six-oared boat, but slimmer and shallower than a sixern

yoag – horse-mussel (Modiolus modiolus), once commonly used as bait

Anyone interested in Shetland Dialect could visit the website of Shetland Forwirds, which includes an online version of John J. Graham's *Shetland Dictionary*, which offers audio clips of individual words.

http://www.shetlanddialect.org.uk/john-j-grahams-shetland-dictionary.php

Acknowledgements

I'm grateful to the editors of the following publications, where some of these poems have appeared. An early version of 'The Puffballs' was published in *Eighteen Bridges*. 'The Ambition' appeared in *Magma* (48) and in Roddy Lumsden's *Best British Poetry 2011*. Some 'Definitions' were published in *poetry london* (76). The poisoned poem, 'The Murder Stone', was commissioned for Alec Finlay and Ken Cockburn's word map of Scotland, 'The Road North', inspired by Basho's *The Narrow Road to the Deep North*. Versions of 'We climb the hill in the dark and the children are finally given back their iPhones' and 'The Session' appear in the *Edinburgh Review* (133).

'Ruined Croft, with Listening Station', 'The Wedding Road, with Free Bar' and 'In Revolution Politics Become Nature' were part of a commission, 'A Highland Romance', for the Manchester Art Gallery and Manchester Literature Festival 2013, which explored Victorian views of Scottishness. 'A Very Circular Song' was written for Pat Law's *Seven Short Sails* project and 'Gloriana' (featuring Mildred) for Alastair Peebles' 'heaps' anthology. John Glenday and I challenged each other to write a poem featuring a piltock (coalfish): the result in my case was 'The White Goods'.

'The Kids' won the Edwin Morgan Poetry Competition in 2012: I'm grateful to the judges, Don Paterson and Gillian Ferguson. Also to the Shetland Library, Shetland Arts and Creative Scotland, for appointing me a Reader-in-Residence in 2012, which was instrumental in providing some much-needed reading and writing time.

A big thank you to Mary Blance for her guidance on Shetland Dialect, and to Alex Cluness, Lilias Fraser, John Glenday, Karen MacKelvie and Malachy Tallack for their feedback on the manuscript.